Praying Through Your Home

Cleaning and Maintaining the Spiritual Environment in Your Home

STEPHANIE BURTON PATTERSON

To my sisters and brothers in Christ
who know that the enemy and
spiritual warfare are both very real
and want to protect their homes
against them.

*The weapons we fight with are not
the weapons of the world. On the
contrary, they have divine power to
demolish strongholds.*
2 Corinthians 10:4 NIV

TABLE OF CONTENTS

"Now My eyes will be open and My ears attentive to prayer made in this place."

2 Chronicles 7:15 NKJ

WHAT'S SO IMPORTANT ABOUT PRAYING THROUGH MY HOME?

Can you imagine what would happen if you never cleaned your house? Not only would dishes and laundry pile up, but think of the dirt, dust, and grime that would accumulate in the bathroom, bedrooms, and living areas! Cleaning your home is essential. Cleaning brings not only sanitation to get rid of dirt, dust, and germs, but it also brings about order in our homes (1 Corinthians 14:40 NIV). Cleaning gives us the chance to organize the chaos that life brings. It gives us a chance to throw out the things we no longer need. Cleaning also helps us to notice when items need to be repaired, updated, or replaced.

Cleaning our homes spiritually essentially does the same thing, only from a spiritual perspective. As we pray through our homes, it gives us a chance to dismiss anything that can cause hindrances and disruptions to the spiritual environment inside our homes (Ephesians 4:31 NLT). It also gives us a chance to pray for the people in our homes as we pray over their personal spaces (Ephesians 6:18 NIV). Praying through our homes gives us the chance to come into agreement with God and align our wills with His regarding our homes and our families.

HOW OFTEN SHOULD I PRAY THROUGH MY HOME?

The official answer is to pray through your home as much as you feel led to (Jeremiah 29:12 GW, 1Chronicles 16:11 NIV, Ephesians 6:18 NIV). Here are some other times you may need to pray through your home:

- You get a new home and want to pray through it before you move in (Matthew 6:33 NLT, Proverbs 24:27 NIV).

- You or family members are having trouble sleeping or with nightmares (Psalm 4:8, Proverbs 3:24 NIV).

- There is discord in your family. This covers the relationships within the house whether it is conflict between spouses, siblings, parents and children, or anyone else living in your home (Ephesians 4:3 NIV, James 3:18 NIV).

- If someone in your house is struggling with stress, discontentment, behavior changes, or other spiritual issues that life circumstances may bring, praying through their personal space is a good idea (1 Peter 5:7 NLT).

- There is a feeling of unrest or disruption or a "weird vibe" in your house (John 1:5 NLT).

- While you physically clean your home, you can pray through it (Colossians 3:23 NIV).

SIX TIPS FOR PRAYING THROUGH YOUR HOME

There are no official rules for doing a prayer walk in your home, but below are some tips:

1. Ask yourself whom you would like to include in the prayer walk. Will you do it by yourself? With a spouse or trusted friend? Maybe consider doing it with adults first to get a feel for it, then maybe include your children another time.

2. There are prayers for both inside and outside your home included in this guide. It is written so that you start praying inside your home and transition to outside your home. Another option is to start outside and end your prayers by praying inside. If that is the case, you would read "Let's Get Started" on page 7, moving to "Outside Prayers" on page 24. From there you are free to follow the remainder of the guide.

3. While this guide recommends that you start at your front door when you are praying inside your house, but you can start anywhere you would like.

4. As you pray in each room, you may want to walk around the room, touching various surfaces: doorknobs, door frames, furniture, countertops, beds, etc. The act of touching can be seen as a form of agreement (Matthew 18:19 KJV), a mechanism for healing and strengthening (Luke 6:19 NIV, Daniel 10:18 NIV), or as a way to anoint or bless an object (Exodus 40:9 NIV).

5. This guide has one prayer for each room in your house, but you may have more than one of the same type of room such as multiple children's rooms or guest rooms. This might lead you to wonder if you say the same prayer for each room. That is up to you. Here are some options:

   - Say the same prayer for each room.

   - Say the same prayer for each room, adding your own personal prayer or scriptures to read. For example, you may have more than one child and each has their own room. You can read the prayer for "Children's Bedrooms" for each room but add scriptures or a special prayer that pertains to each child specifically. This is especially helpful if your child has a specific issue that you want to cover in prayer. There are scriptures that begin on page 48 ("More Scriptures for Your Home and the People in It") that you may want to use, or you may find some on your own. Google is very handy for finding Bible scriptures that pertain to specific issues.

6. You may have other rooms that are not covered in this guide such as a library, music room, sewing room, sunroom, home gym, or another type of room. In those cases, there is an "Additional Rooms" prayer on page 38. If you have specific prayers or prayer needs for those spaces, you have the option of praying them there. If you are looking for scriptures to support those special areas, refer to the scriptures that begin on page 48. As mentioned in the previous step, Google is your friend! Type in "Bible scriptures for" and type in a topic. Here are some examples:

Looking for scriptures for a home library? Try searching using Bible scriptures on books, reading, writing, or knowledge. Music room? Try searching Bible scriptures on music or worship. Home gym? Search body, fitness, run, or race. There are note pages at the end of this guide that make a great place to jot down scriptures that you find, issues that you want to pray about, or general notes you may want to make.

PREPARE FOR YOUR PRAYER WALK

Take a few minutes to prepare yourself before you do the prayer walk around your home. Here are some ways to prepare:

- Quiet your mind. Take some time to breathe—literally. Inhale God's peace and ask Him for focus. As you exhale, think of pushing distractions out of your mind and heart.

- Eliminate digital interruptions. Turn off or silence phones, televisions, etc.

- Go before God with the following prayer:

Our Father in heaven,

Reveal who you are.

Set the world right;

Do what's best—as above, so below.

Keep us alive with three square meals.

Keep us forgiven with You and forgiving others.

Keep us safe from ourselves and the Devil.

You're in charge!

You can do anything you want!

You're ablaze in beauty (Matthew 6:5-18 TMB)!

- Focus on your gratitude to God for giving you this home. Praise Him and thank Him for it. It is truly a blessing (James 1:17 NIV)!

Let's Get Started

Recommendation: Begin the prayer walk through your home in the entryway or on the front porch.

SUGGESTED PRAYER

Matthew chapter 7 (NIV) says that *Everyone who hears my teaching and applies it to his life can be compared to a wise man who built his house on an unshakable foundation* (v. 24). Lord, we pray for our homes to have an unshakable foundation. When the rains fall in our lives, we want to stand firm because of that strong foundation (v. 25). We refuse to be like those who hear Your teaching and do not apply it to their lives, because then our foundations are on sandy, unstable ground and will collapse and be swept away (v.26-27). For this reason, we cover our home today, Lord God.

Lord, Your Word says that we are head and not the tail (Deuteronomy 28:13 NIV). You have given us power to trample over snakes and scorpions (Luke 10:19 NIV). We are grateful to have this authority, simply because we belong to You. We exercise our authority to claim peace in our hearts, minds, and in our home.

Lord, You have given us this home to be stewards of. The Word says that You want to give us the very kingdom itself! Let us not be preoccupied with gaining possessions so that we can respond to Your giving (I John 2:15-17 NLT). People who struggle to trust You fuss over material things. Remind us of that truth when we worry and stress over having the latest and greatest items. Let us *steep our lives in God-reality, God-initiative, God-provisions. We will find all of our everyday human concerns will be met* (Luke 12:29-32 TMB).

As we prepare to pray through our homes, we firmly state that we choose this day whom we will serve; we and our house will serve You, Lord (Joshua 24:15 NIV).

Exterior Doors

Recommendation: As you pray, touch each exterior door, ending with the front door.

SUGGESTED PRAYER

Lord, we pray over the doors of our home. Bless those who arrive at our home, and those who depart from it (Deuteronomy 28:6 NIV). Let people who visit us feel Your love the minute they walk in. Let our home be a place of peace, harmony, and rest in the name of Jesus. Keep evil and those with evil intentions away from our home. Should evil make its way into our home, let it be uncomfortable and unable to stay here. Lord, we ask that You keep watch over us as we come and go out of each door of our home (Psalm121:8 NIV).

Living/Family Room

Recommendation: As you pray, touch doorway, sofa, chairs, etc.

SUGGESTED PRAYER

Lord, bless our living room. It is the place we congregate. It's where we relax with family, friends, and guests. Bless this place. Let this be a place where all the worries of the day dissolve. Here we receive Your peace and turn away from tension and strife.

Let guests feel welcome in our living room, Lord. Your Word says in Romans 12:13 (TPT) that we are to *Take a constant interest in the needs of God's beloved people and respond by helping them, and eagerly welcome people as guests into our home.* Let us embrace this Biblical practice fully as we invite people into our home.

Give us the opportunity to show Your love to our guests and never let us miss a chance to minister to them (Romans 15:16 NIV).

Kitchen

Recommendation: As you pray, touch doorway, counters, table, oven, stove, etc.

SUGGESTED PRAYER

We pray over our kitchen. *The eyes of all look to You in hope; you give them their food as they need it. When You open your hand, You satisfy the hunger and thirst of every living thing* (Psalm 145:15-16 NLT). Lord, we want to be as healthy in body as we are strong in spirit (3 John1:2 NLT). Please bless this place where we store and prepare the food meant for the nourishment of the bodies You have given us. We thank You for being our Provider. We ask You to bless each item we prepare and eat. Let us be good stewards of our health. May the food we purchase help us reach that goal. We ask for creative healthy recipes and foods that will help us not only nourish our bodies, but the bodies of those who we invite into our home.

We ask that You bless the preparing and the eating of bread in this space. Whether we eat or drink, we do all to the glory of God (1 Corinthians 10:31 NLT) for *You satisfy the thirsty and fill the hungry with good things* (Psalm 107:9 NLT).

Dining Room

Recommendation: As you pray, touch doorway, dining table and chairs.

SUGGESTED PRAYER

We pray over our dining room. Your Word speaks of attending temple together and breaking bread in our homes, receiving our food with glad and generous hearts, all the while praising You and enjoying the goodwill of all the people (Acts 2:46 NIV). Your Word also says that each day You add to our fellowship (Acts 2:47 NLT). Let us eat our food with joy, and drink our wine with a happy heart, for You approve of this (Ecclesiastes 9:7 NLT)! Father, we ask these things as we share meals with our family and friends in this space.

Prayer for Pets

Recommendation: Pets are an important part of the family for many people. This prayer can be prayed over the area that your pet sleeps, or where they spend the most time in your home.

SUGGESTED PRAYER

Father, thank You so much for our pet(s). He/She/They is/are a welcome addition to our home. We thank You that he/she/they not only provide us with companionship but add so much to our lives. You use them to model so many attributes that we should have ourselves including loyalty, compassion, unconditional love, and the propensity to listen (Colossians 3:12 NIV, James 1:19 NIV, Proverbs 21:21 NLT). We ask that You keep them healthy and safe. Show us how to properly care for them as they care for us.

Guest Bedrooms

Recommendation: As you pray, touch doorway, bed, furniture, etc.

SUGGESTED PRAYER

We pray, Lord over our guest room. We pray that it is a place where our guests can feel Your peace. As they rest, Father, protect their hearts and guard their minds (Philippians 4:7 NIV). Let the tranquility of the atmosphere created in our home by You permeate their stay here.

Let Your love be felt in our home so that those who know You feel closer to You. Let those who do not know You be curious about what it is that they feel when they are in our home—that feeling of warmth, serenity, and love; that feeling that comes from being in Your presence (Psalm 16:11 NIV). Give us an opportunity to share with and minister to our guests in just the right way so that they can receive what You put on our hearts to share.

Guest Room Closet Prayer: Proverbs 31:21 (NIV) says that the virtuous woman is not afraid of snow for her household, for all her household are clothed in warmth and comfort (scarlet) Let our guests feel the warmth and comfort of our home as they rest here.

Children's Bedrooms

Recommendation: As you pray, touch doorway, bed, furniture, possessions, etc.

SUGGESTED PRAYER

We pray through the rooms of our children. Father, let their rooms be a place of refuge for them. Let their rooms be filled with calm and let their sleep be sweet (Proverbs 3:24 NIV). We pray against any attempt of the enemy to invade this room in any way. We come against any attempt of him to invade our children in any way.

We pray that their identity would be rooted firmly in You, and not in who or what the world says they should be. Our children are in this world, but not of it (John 17:15-19 NIV). Let them not conform to this world but be transformed by the renewing of their mind. As they focus on You, enable them to be wise and discerning as they navigate their lives (Romans 12:2 NIV).

Lord, we can't know everything that goes on with our children but give us wisdom and strength regarding the things we need to know about them whether we discover them on our own, or through other people.

Give us a realistic view of our children, both their strengths and areas they need to improve in. Let us see our children through Your eyes. Show us how to parent each of them exactly the way they need to be parented.

Children's Bedroom Closet Prayer: Lord, let us teach our children that they are so much more than what they wear. Let them be grateful and gracious. We pray against the materialism of our society corrupting their hearts and minds. We pray that they will be clothed with the full armor of God (Ephesians 6:10-18 NIV). Prepare them and us to face whatever each day holds for them.

Owner's Suite

Recommendation: As you pray, touch doorway, bed, furniture, etc.

SUGGESTED PRAYER

Single Owners

Lord, I cover my bedroom. Let this room be my retreat wherein I can unwind, rest, and recharge. Guard my mind from any anxious thoughts in this room. Bless not only this room, but me, Lord. Increase my relationship with You. Your Word says that You will draw nearer to me when I draw nearer to You. Help me to make not only my relationship with You a priority but help me to make Your Word a priority as well (James 4:8 NIV, Matthew 22:37-38 NIV, Psalm 119:10-11 NLT).

Married Owners

Lastly, we pray over our bedroom. Let this be a place of connection; where we hear each other and listen to each other's needs. Good rest should happen here. Here we are protected from the reaches of the enemy as we restore, recharge, and reconnect together each evening. Bless not only this room, but this marriage. Strengthen our connection to each other and to You.

Owner's Suite Closet Prayer: Lord, clothes are but one thing we need provision for. As I/we dress for work, let me/us not be anxious for You are our provider. You provide for the ravens. They are unfettered, not tied down to a job description, and worry free in Your care. And we, as Your children count far more (Luke 12:22-24 TMB). Your Word says that there is far more to our lives than the clothes we hang on our bodies. It reminds us that *wildflowers don't fuss with their appearance—but we have never seen color and design quite like them. In fact, the ten best-dressed men and women in the country look shabby alongside them. So, if You give such attention to the wildflowers, You will attend to us, take pride in us, and do Your best for us* (Luke 25-28 TMB).

Bathrooms

Recommendation: As you pray, touch doorway, and sink top.

SUGGESTED PRAYER

Father, we ask You to bless our bathrooms. These are the rooms in which we not only clean and prepare ourselves for the day that lies ahead of us, but also where we wash the day off us as we prepare to rest. Lord, You tell us in Your Word that You will bring us in and sprinkle clean water on us and we will be clean (Ezekiel 36:25 NIV). Lord, as we begin our day or end our day in this room, let us not only be clean on the outside, but also clean on the inside. Remind us to clean our hearts by forgiving others, confessing our sins, and remembering our many blessings (Psalm 51:10 NIV). We pray that we will be as diligent about cleaning, preparing, caring for, and adorning our spirits as we are our outer bodies.

Laundry Room

Recommendation: As you pray, touch doorway, washer, dryer, etc.

SUGGESTED PRAYER

Revelation 22:14 (NIV) says, "Blessed are those who wash their robes, so that they may have the right to the tree of life and may enter by the gates into the city." The same way we decide when it is time to wash our clothes, help us decide to evaluate our lives, identifying any area that we need to clean up. Create in us a clean heart (Psalm 51:10 NLT). Show us any areas that have hidden stains and let us rely on You to help us remove them. Father, we ask that You remind us that what we clothe ourselves in physically is not nearly as important as the way we clothe ourselves spiritually. Man looks at the outer appearance, but You look at the heart (1 Samuel 16:7 NLT).

Home Office

Recommendation: As you pray, touch doorway, desk, chairs, computer, etc.

SUGGESTED PRAYER

Bless and establish the work of our hands (Deuteronomy 28:12 NIV, Psalm 90:17 NIV). Let our ideas flow freely. Let the work we do glorify You.

Help us be a light to the people we work with and serve alongside. Help us also be a light for those we work for, as well as those who work under us (Matthew 5:14 NIV).

Lord, we also pray to be good stewards over all you have entrusted us with; our jobs, our finances, our time, and even our volunteer opportunities (1 Corinthians 4:2 NLT).

We pray for productivity in this room and in our lives. Let Your favor rest upon us.

Additional Rooms

Recommendation: As you pray, touch doorway, furniture, etc.

SUGGESTED PRAYER

Lord, we ask for Your blessings to be in this room. We pray for the purpose of this room. Let all that we do here be glorifying to You (1 Corinthians 10:31 NIV). Let Your eyes be open and ears attentive to the prayers that are made in this place. Choose and consecrate this room and let Your name be in this room. May Your ears and heart be present at all times (2 Chronicles 7:15-16 NLT).

Attic, Basement, Garage

Recommendation: As you pray, touch doors, cars, furniture, etc.

*If your basement, attic, or garage is used as a finished living space and has some of the same rooms as the main part of your home (bedrooms, kitchen, living area, etc.), the same prayers as you prayed for those rooms in the house apply there.

SUGGESTED PRAYER

Let this prayer cover the other areas of our house: the attic, garage, and basement. Whether these are areas we use often or rarely, they are the places where we store our possessions. We thank You for the provision of these possessions, but we do not place their importance over our need for You, the supplier of all our needs according to Your riches and glory (Philippians 4:19 NIV).

Help us keep the possessions You bless us with in perspective. They belong to You; we are merely stewards of them. Let us never be owned by our possessions, and never let us lose sight of the fact that they are gifts from You, as You have given us the ability to work and save for these things we possess. While we do not place the value of "stuff" over our need for You, we still ask for Your presence to cover these areas fully.

Home Operation Systems- Lord, since the mechanics of our homes are often stored in or near these places, we ask for Your covering over our home's operational networks (fuse box, hot water heater, furnace, air conditioners, internet, etc). The same way that You designed our bodily systems to work together so that our whole body functions as it should, may our house systems work together to make our home run efficiently and comfortably. Let each system in our home plays its part contributing to the smooth running of the whole (1 Corinthians 12:14 NIV, Ephesians 4:16 NIV).

Vehicles- Father, we also pray over our vehicles- cars, boats, bicycles, RVs, campers, motorcycles, and any other machine we rely on for transportation whether we use them daily or for leisure. We ask for the wisdom and financial ability to maintain these vehicles. We ask for safe travels for not only our family members who use these vehicles, but anyone riding in or on them. Your Word says that You will order Your angels to protect us wherever we go (Psalm 91:11 NLT). We pray for safety and protection against collisions and calamity.

God, we ask for Your hedge of protection over each of these spaces, systems, and possessions.

Outdoor Prayers

Recommendation: As you pray, walk around the perimeter of the property and around deck or patio.

SUGGESTED PRAYER

Father, we pray for the outside of our home. Bless it from the rooftop to the foundation and the ground below it. We ask for protection against natural disasters and severe weather. Let this house, which has You as its foundation stand firm against the elements. Give us wisdom in the maintenance of our homes.

Front and back yards - Lord, we ask that Your protection of our home extend to each border of our property. Your Word says that You make peace in our borders and that violence will not be heard in our land, nor devastation or destruction within our borders (Psalm 147:14 NIV, Isaiah 60:18 NIV). You placed Adam and Eve in the Garden of Eden to cultivate it and to keep it (Genesis 2:15 NLT). Lord, this yard is our Eden. Let us maintain it and make You proud as it is the face of the home you have given us. We ask You to bless the very ground itself. May all that we plant grow and prosper. Give us wisdom in the care of our yard.

Patio/Deck- Lord, we cover our patio/deck/porch areas. Let these be our areas of outdoor relaxation. Give us an appreciation of Your creativity and the great care You take in making each aspect of nature (Colossians 1:16 NIV).

Neighbors-We also pray for our neighbors. Your Word calls us to love our neighbors as ourselves (Mark 12:31 NLT). Lord, Your Word also calls us to live in peace with our neighbors (Romans 12:18 NLT). We pray for good relationships with our neighbors and that we live peacefully with them.

Let us never miss a chance for Your character to be reflected in us. We want to be Your hands and feet when those around us need help (I Corinthians 12:27 NIV). Help us have the thoughts and actions of the good Samaritan where our neighbors are concerned (Luke 10:29-37 NLT). Let our servant's hearts ultimately draw our neighbors to You (Philippians 2:3-5 NLT).

Closing Prayers

Recommendation: Close your prayer in the same place you started, or in a place of your choice.

SUGGESTED PRAYER

We take complete authority and dominion over this home in Your Son Jesus' name, Lord. Anything that is in any corner of this house that is not of You does not belong here, and we cast it out in the name of Jesus.

We fully stand on Your Word which states, *if we make the Lord our refuge, if we make the Most High our shelter, no evil will conquer us; no plague or disaster will come near our home* (Psalm 91:9-10 NIV).

We pray, according to Your Word, that our home would be a peaceful dwelling place, a secure home, an undisturbed place of rest. Protect this house from the rooftop to the foundation, from wall to wall, from nail to nail. Thank You, Lord. Amen!

MORE SCRIPTURES FOR YOUR HOME (AND THE PEOPLE IN IT)

Here are some other scriptures that you may want to use as you pray over your home and/or family members. They are also great scriptures to commit to memory and to meditate on.

Scriptures on Peace

- *May peace be within your walls, And prosperity within your palaces.* Psalm 122:7 NLT

- *Be joyful. Grow to maturity. Encourage each other. Live in harmony and peace. Then the God of love and peace will be with you.* 2 Corinthians 13:11 NLT

- *When I am afraid, I put my trust in you.* Psalms 56:3 NIV

- *Do not be anxious about anything, but in every situation, by prayer and petition, with thanksgiving, present your requests to God.*

And the peace of God, which transcends all understanding, will guard your hearts and your minds in Christ Jesus. Philippians 4:6-7 NIV

- *May God, who gives this patience and encouragement, help you live in complete harmony with each other, as is fitting for followers of Christ Jesus.* Romans 15:5 NLT

- *When you enter a house, first say, 'Peace to this house!'* Luke 10:5 NIV

Scriptures on Rest/Sleep

- *When you lie down, you will not be afraid; when you lie down, your sleep will be sweet.* Proverbs 3:24 NIV

- *In peace I will lie down and sleep, for you alone, O Lord, will keep me safe.* Psalm 4:8 NLT

- *Whoever dwells in the shelter of the Most High will rest in the shadow of the Almighty.* Psalm 91:1 NIV

- *I lie down and sleep; I wake again, because the LORD sustains me.* Psalm 3:5 NIV

- *Return to your rest, my soul, for tthe Lord has been good to you.* Psalm 116:7 NIV

Scriptures on Gratitude

- *Give thanks to the Lord, for he is good! His faithful love endures forever! - Psalm 136:1* NLT

- *Now, our God, we give you thanks, and praise your glorious name.* 1 Chronicles 29:13 NIV

- *Give thanks in all circumstances; for this is God's will for you in Christ Jesus.* 1 Thessalonians 5:18 NIV

- *This is the day the LORD has made. We will rejoice and be glad in it.* Psalm 118:24 NLT

Scriptures on Encouragement

- *But those who hope in the Lord will renew their strength. They will soar on wings like eagles; they will run and not grow weary, they will walk and not be faint.* Isaiah 41:30 NIV

- *If God is for us, who can ever be against us?* Romans 8:31 NLT

- *I know the Lord is always with me. I will not be shaken, for he is right beside me.* Psalm 16:8 NLT

- *Be strong and take heart, all you who hope in the Lord.* Psalm 31:24 NIV

- *God is our refuge and strength, always ready to help in times of trouble.* Psalm 46:1 NLT

Scriptures on Conquering Fear, Anxiety, Stress

- *For God has not given us a spirit of fear, but of power and of love and of a sound mind.* 2 Timothy 1:7 NKJ

- *I will say of the LORD, "He is my refuge and my fortress, my God, in whom I trust."* Psalm 91:2 NIV

- *Come to me, all you who are weary and burdened, and I will give you rest.* Matthew 11:28 NIV

- *Have I not commanded you? Be strong and courageous. Do not be afraid; do not be discouraged, for the Lord your God will be with you wherever you go.* - Joshua 1:9 NIV

- *Do not be afraid or discouraged, for the Lord will personally go ahead of you. He will be with you; he will neither fail you nor abandon you.* Deuteronomy 31:8 NLT

- *Trust in the Lord with all your heart; do not depend on your own understanding. Seek his will in all you do, and he will show you which path to take.* Proverbs 3:5-6 NIV

- *I praise God for what he has promised. I trust in God, so why should I be afraid? What can mere mortals do to me?* Psalm 56:4 NLT

- *The Lord is my light and my salvation-whom shall I fear? The Lord is the stronghold of my life-of whom shall I be afraid?* Psalm 27:1 NIV

- *I prayed to the Lord, and he answered me. He freed me from all my fears.* Psalm 34:4 NIV

- *Surely the righteous will never be shaken; they will be remembered forever. They will have no fear of bad news; their hearts are steadfast, trusting in the Lord. Their hearts are secure, they will have no fear;* Psalm 112:6-8a NIV

Scriptures on God's Protection

- *As for God, His way is perfect. The Word of the LORD is proven. He is a shield to all those who take refuge in Him.* Psalm 18:30 NKJ

- *For you are my hiding place; you protect me from trouble. You surround me with songs of victory.* Psalm 32:7 NLT

- *Have mercy on me, O God, have mercy! I look to you for protection. I will hide beneath the shadow of your wings until the danger passes by.* Psalm 57:1 NLT

- *He will not let you stumble; the one who watches over you will not slumber.* Psalm 121:3 NLT

- *The LORD Himself watches over you! The LORD stands beside you as your protective shade.* Psalm 121:5 NLT

- *The LORD keeps you from all harm and watches over your life.* Psalm 121:7 NLT

- *The LORD keeps watch over you as you come and go, both now and forever.* Psalm 121:8 NLT

- *Every word of God proves true. He is a shield to all who come to Him for protection.* Proverbs 30:5 NLT

- *I will say of the LORD, "He is my refuge and my fortress, my God, in whom I trust."* Psalm 91:2 NIV

- *If you make the Lord your refuge, if you make the Most High your shelter, no evil will conquer you; no plague will come near your home. For he will order his angels to protect you wherever you go.* Psalm 91:9-11 NLT

- *Be strong and courageous. Don't tremble! Don't be afraid of them! The LORD your God is the one who is going with you. He won't abandon you or leave you.* Deuteronomy 31:6 GW

- *Don't be afraid, for I am with you. Don't be discouraged, for I am your God. I will strengthen you and help you. I will hold you up with my victorious right hand.* Isaiah 41:10 NLT

- *But let all who take refuge in you rejoice. Let them sing with joy forever. Protect them, and let those who love your name triumph in you.* Psalm 5:11 GW

- *The LORD says, "I will rescue those who love Me. I will protect those who trust in My name."* Psalm 91:14 NLT

- *God is our refuge and strength, always ready to help in times of trouble.* Psalms 46:1 NLT

- *Rescue me from my enemies, O my God.*

- *Protect me from those who attack me.* Psalm 59:1 NLT

- *Protect me from the hands of wicked people, O Lord. Keep me safe from violent people. They try to trip me.* Psalm 140:4 GW

- *Rescue me and free me because of Your righteousness. Turn Your ear toward me and save me.* Psalm 71:2 GW

- *He said, The Lord is my rock and my fortress and my Savior, my God, my rock in whom I take refuge, my shield, the strength of my salvation, my stronghold, my refuge, and my Savior who saved me from violence.* 2 Samuel 22:2-3 GW

- *Even when I walk through the darkest valley, I will not be afraid, for you are close beside me.*

- *Your rod and your staff protect and comfort me.* Psalm 23:4 NLT

- *Be my rock of refuge, to which I can always go; give the command to save me, for you are my rock and my fortress.* Psalm 71:3 NIV

NOTES

53

Writing things down is an excellent way to remember and record your thoughts. Use this area to take notes on:

- Issues that happen with yourself or family members that require prayer.

- Praise reports and answers to prayer.

- Prayers of your own that you may have for your home or family members.

- It can also be used to record scriptures that you want to use in your prayers.

NOTES

NOTES

NOTES

NOTES

NOTES

NOTES

NOTES

NOTES

NOTES

NOTES

63